THE LATE SUN

by the same author

poetry
ARCADIA
PEA SOUP
KATERINA BRAC
IN THE ECHOEY TUNNEL
EXPANDED UNIVERSES
FOR AND AFTER
MR MOUTH
THE SONG OF LUNCH
SELECTED POEMS
NONSENSE
SIX BAD POETS
THE CURIOSITIES
A SCATTERING and ANNIVERSARY

for children
ALL SORTS
ALPHABICYCLE ORDER
OLD TOFFER'S BOOK OF CONSEQUENTIAL DOGS

as editor
SOUNDS GOOD: 101 Poems to Be Heard
NOT TO SPEAK OF THE DOG: 101 Short Stories in Verse
LETTERS OF TED HUGHES

CHRISTOPHER REID

The Late Sun

faber

First published in 2020
by Faber & Faber Ltd
Bloomsbury House
74–77 Great Russell Street
London WC1B 3DA
This paperback edition first published in 2021

Typeset by Hamish Ironside
Printed in the UK by TJ Books Ltd, Padstow, Cornwall

A CIP record for this book is available from the British Library

ISBN 978-0-571-36025-3

10 9 8 7 6 5 4 3 2 1

Contents

Photography

With the time at an hour to lunch,
the restaurant door stands open.
Not taking its welcome for granted,
the sun has stepped in at a diffident
angle – one pace, no further –
and waits to grow slowly less slanted.

Beyond it, tables are poised.
Laundered and starched, their cloths
give them the calm, reassuring
air of disciplined nurses.
Ranked cutlery, upside-down glasses
and unsoiled side-plates
are serenely composed, enduring.

All human fuss is backstage,
with the simmering sauces and menus
perhaps even now being written.
What I can see and am smitten
by is a cool, square depth
of shadow and nuance,
fixed for an instant, an age.

Arboristics

Less limber than a lemur,
    which enjoys the unfair advantage
of an infinitely elastic,
    imaginary harness
as it grope-lopes through the jungle,
    tugging and twanging branches,

the tree surgeon keeps to one tree
    at a time, a London plane –
from a roadside single file
    of council-owned London planes,
now due for a trim and tidy-up;
    hence, his swaying and belaying

twenty feet above stopped traffic:
    just a job; and yet his antics
have drawn a circus audience,
    so daredevilishly he dangles,
riproaring with his chainsaw;
    and we're both amused and anxious

as we wait below to see
    the upshot of his lopping:
whether some big branch or he
    will come spectacularly dropping,
and our vehicles be free
    at last to stop their stopping.

Running at the Sea

They run at the sea, the sea runs at them,
small girl, smaller boy,
silhouetted against the setting sun.

They are of the age of jutting bellies
and rounded behinds,
the rest of them slender, tensile.

When she leans forward to start her run,
she's a hunter,
halted, alert, in an African rock painting.

Standing, he's Etruscan;
pointing at distance, in profile,
a much-photographed museum Giacometti.

They run at the sea, the sea keeps running at them.

They skip the front rank
of minor, expiring waves,
crash shin-deep, thigh-deep, into the next,

then either retreat
or meet the body-blow of the rollers
with a stunned stagger, involuntary spin,

or full, backward collapse.

When the sea withdraws,
they leap up and run back to the shore
to do it all over again:

the running, the skipping, the crashing and collapsing.

Their voices are too far off to be heard;
we hear only the sea
running to greet and defeat them

with its eternal turmoil of boom and shush.

Mountains

Mountains had crept up
under the wing of the plane.

I must have nodded off
not to have felt their approach.

Spurning daylight, their darkness
was what alerted me.

An encampment of lugubrious
giants helmeted in ice!

Our altitude made them crouch
but could not diminish their menace.

Sun, commanding from the rear,
bestowed superficial glitter.

More, though, it enhanced
the sheer drops, chasms, vertigos.

Inhospitable valleys
hiding their inhabitants, if any.

Communities of boulders
banished to eternal shadow.

Echoes forever waiting to happen;
if happening, unheard.

Geology and time
at their most savage and slovenly.

Not a region for the tidy
or timid mind to dwell on;

nor for a plane to slacken
cruising speed over.

Sophie among the Elements

i.m. Sophie Milburn

We were new, or newish, friends
walking with other friends
along the beach at Aldeburgh,
when, without preamble, she stopped,
stepped aside and stripped
down to bathing togs
we had no idea she'd been wearing
under her autumn clothing;
then, lean and single-purposed
as a lurcher chasing a hare,
she raced for the chill North Sea –
which met her with an embrace
that would have done for me –
while we all stood and gazed,
amazed, admiring.

That wasn't her only difference:
as I grew to understand,
she lived among the elements –
water to swim in or sail;
earth from which she raised
gardens in her own style
of bounty and beauty;
fire for the alchemical
transformation of clay,
or impromptu magicking-up
of lavish, delicious meals –
with an ease and intimacy
few others could match.

And air? Think of her voice:
that diffident mumble
often so hard to catch
before it fled into thin air,
like the air that surrounds us today
and from which we strain
to clarify and retain
of one so close to the elements
a full-bodied memory.

The Frost-Fox

A fox, a dainty young vixen,
        lay on my mother's lawn, dead.
She lay on her left side, frozen
        mid-trot, as if targeted
by Death the Sniper – hidden
        among the trees, or crouched overhead

on the bungalow roof. January
        frost had struck and silvered
the garden all over, every
        grass-blade, leaf and twig. Nothing stirred.
The effect was both pretty and eerie,
        like some enchantment suffered

in a fairy tale. The fox, also,
        had lain there long enough
to begin to undergo
        transmutation: outer hairs stiff
with glitter, while the rich pelt below
        remained the colour of snuff;

a sparkle added to the white
        of the muzzle. No wound visible.
Her upper lip lifted in a tight,
        toothy sneer showed how contemptible
she considered this impolite
        interruption, and resembled

a look that had crossed
        my mother's face as she lay dying
not three months past.
        I couldn't keep the creature lying
like that. Working fast,
        I was soon plying

a spade in the hard earth
        at the back of the garden.
Job done, all that was left
        was the grass-green silhouette of a vixen
nimbly stepping forth
        to meet her fortune.

A Bungalow in West Byfleet

Questions I never thought to ask
and questions I thought to ask but never did –
equally futile, equally pressing –
are heavy in the air of this, your last
and longest home. Oh, and yes:
let me not omit from my accounting
questions I asked, to which I have forgotten the answers.

You volunteered so little of your past:
bare facts, with how things struck you at the time
and what you felt about them now
mainly left out; your ninety-four years
wrapped up in a reticence
which wasn't, I don't suppose, designed to keep us
    guessing,
more a generation thing, a habit of making light.

Born in West Ham – I believe I've got that right –
you started your world-wandering early,
carried off in your cradle to Hong Kong,
where your father served as a prison officer.
Of William Dedear's
appearance, character, achievements,
I know next to nothing. Not a single photograph
    survives.

Then your childhood: to me, a fast-forward blur,
ending at the Japanese invasion
and the family's upheaval to Australia. What followed
sounds fun. Picnics with young chaps in uniform.
A job that allowed you to buy your own piano.
Wartime liberties. But before long
you're back in the colony, resuming your interrupted life.

Wedding day: a sudden accumulation
of photographs, glamorous bride and bridesmaids
caught in a swirl of veils and lace; groom, too, in white.
Honeymoon snaps. Christenings. Cocktail parties,
nobody without a cigarette. Then Daddy's career
that took you both to the Middle East, Africa, Asia –
anywhere, so long as it was warm.

Such a sweep of travelling, but it had to alight
somewhere, and so it did, after widowhood,
at this bric-à-brac-filled bungalow,
which it's now the task of your dithering son to clear.
What to save and what to give away,
what to condemn to the dump: too many
treacherous, heart-tugging, heart-breaking choices!

Is this what a life amounted to? No,
and let's not even talk in terms of 'amounting',
even though I could wish there were less
of a deficit on my side. Still, I'll take a few things home –
the albums, that ebony elephant,
your Ethiopian *Queen of Sheba* painting –
in the hope of going some way towards making good.

Two on the Edge

Two on the edge of a landing strip
stand poised for some romantic trip.

Honeymoon I'd guess it to be,
from their unpractised intimacy.

He, three-piece-suited, braced and trim,
accepts her leaning into him.

Hair waved in post-war Hollywood style
falls either side of her shy smile.

Behind them, a small passenger plane,
nose tilted, waits to take off again.

But first, the photographer – no idea who –
must catch this moment and keep it new,

against the years into which they flew.

Chinoiserie

for Tim and Carolyn

Fifties Epsom: we were a family
distinguished (or made less inconspicuous)
by a red-framed signboard at the foot of our driveway:
'Fan Ling', in both Chinese and Roman characters,
under a green, pagoda-style canopy.

As if we were a misplaced Cantonese restaurant!
Indoors, one wall of the dining room
was hung with another import from Hong Kong,
pagoda-pattern paper – until the plumbing succumbed
to English freeze/burst, and the whole panorama had to
    come down.

In photographs, our gentle amah, Ah Fook,
stands with us out in the garden, stiff with posing
and with the shock of the cold, snowflakes
blobbing all around. Hardly surprising
that in short time she took the boat back to her own
    folk.

Touches of chinoiserie were everywhere:
pictures, porcelain bowls, embroidered table linen,
fiddly carvings in bone or ivory:
our mother's smugglings into an alien
Home Counties environment, and focus for nostalgic
    reverie?

Not exactly. Rather, they were signs
of a singular identity, carried from house to house
for the rest of her long life. Her Chineseness
I'd call it, if it didn't sound incorrect or grandiose.
But hang on, why not? That was the essence –

embodied now in the carved camphor-wood
chest I asked her to bequeath me,
with the galloping horseman on the lid.
I raise it and the whoomph of camphor rises to greet me,
just as in childhood it did.

A Summoning of Proper Nouns

The big, smart P&O Building was where they lived:
offices below, flats above, and the globally recognised
    initials
high up on the left-hand side as you approached it.
My father worked for Shell, another firm with a well-
    travelled logo,
in an office I don't remember ever visiting.
Their flat was on the third floor, reached by a lift,
spacious, and ready to greet you with the merciful chill
    of air-conditioning.
A long verandah at the front of the building
surveyed a patch of ground – grassless, obviously –
where soccer was played by lanky, loose-limbed Somali
    lads,
who, if they happened not to have a ball,
used the goalpost crossbars as casual gym equipment
until one turned up. A mosque, somewhere beyond,
broadcast calls to prayer. Grey mountains beyond that.
At the back of the building lay the harbour,
busy with the to and fro of international shipping:
grand liners – P&O, Union Castle – and oil tankers,
    principally,
as this was before the closure of the Suez Canal,
all with the diligent attendance of grubby tugs and pilot
    boats.
Front and back were where the world went on, endlessly
    watchable.
Between them, another sort of life: Sobranie Cocktail
    cigarettes
fragrantly waiting in cloisonné boxes to be offered to
    guests;

a drinks cabinet from which my father occasionally
    mixed
a Curried Gin, his own invention – gin, ice, several jolts
    of Tabasco,
and a skewered cocktail onion where an olive might
    have been;
for everyday, Oranjeboom, pronounced in the English
    manner,
poured foaming to the top of long glasses, while we
    children
made ourselves giddy on Coke or Fanta; within hand's
    reach,
Norman Rockwell gracing the cover of the *Saturday
    Evening Post*,
syndicated Andy Capp and Dagwood Bumstead
towards the back of the local rag, whose name escapes
    me,
'It Pays to Increase Your Word Power' in the *Reader's
    Digest*;
Never on Sunday or *My Fair Lady* spinning on the
    turntable;
Shelltox, the firm's product, snatched up to squirt and
    poison the air
whenever a fly was brash enough to burst on the scene;
no TV, but the Sony 'Earth-Orbiter', which every
    evening
brought 'Lillibullero' and the World Service news to
    anyone listening.

Actual Age

You were meant to look double
your actual age,
when you starred as Miss Marple
in *Murder at the Vicarage*.

Old-lady make-up,
talc to whiten your hair,
and a stagey stoop
brought you nowhere near.

Still, we were delighted
to watch our mother
standing in for Margaret Rutherford
for one big night.

An odd play to put on
in oven-top Aden,
even for homesick
ex-pats in the sixties.

Required to perform
in tweeds, trilbies, overcoats,
your supporting cast
must have been – well, *warm*.

Never mind: you were all
flying the flag:
chin up and unflagging
till curtain call.

~

In actual,
unacted age,
you appeared to manage
pretty well,
even debonairly,
with shopping trolley
as your prop
and walking-frame,
both at the shops
and back home;
but that was show,
a bright performance
meant to disguise
arthritic pains
and other frailties
unbecoming
an independent woman
in her nineties,
full of go
and other qualities
carried over
from an earlier stage
of relished life,
a not quite bygone age.

Unheard Words

The stroke foretold by your consultant struck
next day. It did not take you long to die.
But first, ordeal by speechlessness, enforced
banishment from all language, punishment
borne with fresh, brave shots at the stubborn,
stuttering silences that kept your thoughts unuttered.
Attempts to write them down were also stumped,
your ballpoint tickling the notepad page with a feeble
image or doodle of your brain's deep damage.
At each failed go, a modest smile of baffled
endeavour, as if this game could be played forever.
It could not, though. The last morning I called,
all words, all thoughts, were hushed, as, turned towards
the wall, you slept. I whispered my farewell.

Kandy

I can't say that I saw the Tooth itself,
but I did see the bedizened elephant that carried it –
as important a performer, surely, as Chesterton's
   donkey –
and hear the clamour and trumpeting
of the accompanying throng.

Our balcony was high above the road
along which the procession passed like a turbulent river
bearing away an unseen holy relic,
bearing elephants, bearing everything away.

Game Theory at Newton Abbot

Two little girls are engaged
in a game of giggles:
a game without rules, or with rules
they invent as they go along.

One throws out, as a challenge,
a scat of high notes; the other
replies in kind, only
higher, wilder, at greater length, or more shrill.

Are they sisters? Friends?
Or just two little girls
flung together in a public place, a railway station,
by another of life's imponderable caprices?

Whoever they are, they are cleverly
making the most of the moment,
enraptured by it, caught up and made giddy
as if by something fast and centrifugal at a fairground.

In this clash and collaboration,
parents, guardians, grown-ups –
we, with our travel plans, tickets, and too much luggage –
cease to exist. Giggling is everything.

Heraclitus in Bishop's Stortford

i.m. Ron Costley

You have to look for it,
but somewhere in the garden
there is a learned stone
that, quoting Heraclitus,
tells you, 'Nature loves to hide.'

Good design
loves to hide, too –
and in the same place.
This is a secret
known to the entire garden.

Another stone, a grave marker,
Latin and lapidary,
remembers a family cat;
a wall plaque invokes
arabesques of swifts.

You recognise the work
of a man of letters,
cultivated, cultivating,
a master of margins
and the typography of flowers.

Self-effacingly,
he made it his purpose
to give pleasure to the seasons.
Turning the pages,
they never read
the same garden twice.

In Memoriam Elliott Carter

Exit, aged 103,
     that amazing mind:
imaginer and creator
     of transcendent scores,
unangry Prospero
     conjuring tempests
from the ordinary orchestra –
     music a supernova
might be happy to dance to,
     free of regular beat,
discontinuous
     in blurts, wisps
and collisions of percussion,
     dimensions clashing,
time at cross-purposes
     with itself,
the whole jingbang
     of genesis and entropy
made palpable
     to the listening
and enraptured pulse.
     Exit, too,
the small, neat,
     tweedy gentleman
occasionally sighted
     in London concert halls,
presenting his merry smile
     like a shield
to left and to right,
     but never disclosing
the secret knowledge whereby

as he grew older
his music travelled
in the opposite direction.

Le Tombeau de Ravel

Musing on his own 'masterpiece', *Boléro* –
'Unfortunately, there's no music in it' –
Ravel reveals himself my kind of hero.

Astounding certainty. What, *no* music? Zero!
More than the witticism of a minute,
this belittling of his world-famous *Boléro*.

The dandy's provocations defy fear. Oh,
to be modest, or self-mocking, and to mean it . . .
For this alone, he can be counted a hero.

A snazzy dresser, dapper as a sparrow,
and, like that pert city bird, minute,
why shouldn't he pop his overblown *Boléro*?

His gift was more for wafts of habanera,
louche blues, corybantic waltz, soured minuet:
forms he explored alone, a dauntless hero.

A paradox, a sort of modernist Pierrot,
mannered, but happy, too, to be rough-mannered –
both composer and disparager of *Boléro* –
Ravel is, let me repeat, my kind of hero!

Death of a Barber

Not Mustafa, but one of his colleagues
cut my hair today.
That's when I learned that Mustafa
had passed away,
a victim of the virus.

Intimate work, the barber's:
fingers, scissors and razor
titivating
with professional gentleness
crown, sides, back and neck.
Almost a caress.

I had been going for ages
to the little shop he used to have,
festooned with climbing plants
and budgerigars in cages,
before I learned Mustafa's name
and something of his life;
but, as etymology tells us,
touch and tact are the same.

For months now, no one had touched me
except my wife,
and I was looking forward
to a needed trim.
I got one, as expert and luxurious
as any of Mustafa's,
but it was not from him.

White Bicycles

In London, these days, a not uncommon sight,
but something Mexican-macabre about it all the same:
lashed to a post, or to railings, a bicycle painted entirely
  white –
white handlebars and frame,
white gears, brakes, wheels, spokes, pedals and chain –
and decked with florists' bunches, satin-bowed and in
  cellophane.
There may be cards and messages as well. Toys, too.
Often a doll or a teddy.
But it's the white that's so striking. What does it mean
  to you?
Ghostliness? A skeleton? (A bicycle being skeletal
  already.)

Oh, get over it, it's the vernacular now; and what's not
  to like
about 'Out with the whited sepulchre! In with the
  whited bike!'?

Magnolia

I have it on good authority
that the Buddha's tree wasn't the Bo Tree
(whatever the Bo Tree may be),
but a front-garden magnolia
from Greater London, or Suburbia.

Should you happen to meet one in full bloom,
there is (again, I'm told) a form
of meditation to observe.
You don't just go *Om*.

Facing the tree, you must raise each arm,
open hands, spread fingers, and become
the very thing you're looking at:
every upward curve
loaded with as much – no, *more*
beauty than it can reasonably bear.

Sketch of a Sketch

for Beverley Bie Brahic

Early, dazzling, cold
October morning:
a young man – or not old –
sits under a café awning.

He tilts back his cappuccino,
gives his moustache a wipe,
then lifts from his jacket pocket
a surprisingly curly pipe
and a plump packet
containing tobacco.

Bowl filled and tamped, match struck
and fluttered above the bowl,
the man begins to suck,
and smoke to roll.
He seems happy, on the whole.

He makes me happy, at least,
and if I were a painter – say,
a 1910 *Intimiste* –
I'd catch him straight away,
him and the lyrical day
that produced this moment.

Words are too quick to comment,
explain, belittle, traduce.
What's the use?
Let me leave this indolent bloke
to his sunlight and smoke.

Smells of London

8 a.m., and a rich pong
thickens the air,
a mulch of stinks suggesting
the binmen have been here
with their cavernous, omnidigesting,
rear-end-fed truck,
which must now be growling along
some nearby street
and gorging on the bagged muck
of your anonymous neighbours.
Try not to mind
if, in the course of its labours,
it leaves behind
a spoor so putrid it's almost sweet.

∾

Wafts out of the blue
the acrid and smutty whiff
of an unabashed outdoor spliff,
and you wonder who
on this well-behaved street
the law-breaker could be.
That builder? One of those three
schoolgirls? The gent with the neat
comb-over? The young mum pacifying
the bundle in her buggy?
No, whoever it was, they've flown
off on some druggy

escapade of their own,
and could still be flying.

☙

Burly air
of barbecue
rolls towards you
across the tops
of fences and hedges:
hint of scorched burgers and chops,
sticky-sauced ribs, sausages
spitting and splitting . . .
Booze-amplified
chatter and laughter
follow soon after.
Then music. Now decide
whether or not to remain sitting
in your garden chair.

☙

Without warning,
an unprovoked, blind-side
stab of recall
from olden days:
pub doors open wide
mid-morning,
not in welcome
but to belch out the foul air –
brew of sour slops,

last night's fag-haze
and general masculine hum –
whereupon the penny drops
on your proneness to feel,
if you don't take care,
the nostalgic appeal
of almost anything at all.

∾

Evening rush hour.
The mob and mesh
of humanity on the hoof,
going home, going out.
From which a scent you know
and can name – *Calèche* –
detaches itself and brushes you lightly.
More whisper than shout,
its mnemonic power
is instant, though,
and you're not memory-proof.
So don't hang about!
Look sprightly!

∾

Almost French
in its cloacal frankness,
a wince-provoking stench
of malfunctioning drains
quickens your stride.

Such point-blankness
can be scary;
but, when it wanes
and you're back to strolling,
reflect with pride
on the great, brick, Victorian torrents rolling
beneath your feet –
as hidden and legendary
as Westbourne or Fleet.

＄

Garlic huffed into your face
by the next straphanger along,
or booming out of the ventilator
of some family restaurant,
reminds you of the pace
of progress since you were young
and new to this place,
then so much drabber, dingier, danker.
Some decades later,
it's a true cosmopolis
and garlic, the lingua franca,
is on everybody's tongue,
everybody's kiss!

Boomers

Every summer, more and more
enormous male babies
waddle out on to the streets.

More and more, larger and larger,
and, by some freak of ageing,
babier and babier.

Once, they were captains of their prime:
strapping lads,
striding and straddling.

Physical labour, military drill,
or rigours of the gym
had made them so.

But time has worked its cruel reverses
and they are humbled,
muscle fallen to flab.

Here's one in comical baseball cap,
shapeless T-shirt
and huge, flapping shorts.

Hands jutting either side
of his tubby trunk
paddle him to the playground of the pub.

Another gawps at sunlight,
which bends to kiss his baldness
as if he had just been lifted from his cot.

Summer, be gentle with your baby boys
learning a world
that they are soon to leave.

Bookshop at Night

for Jen Campbell

Lights out, security grille
drawn down, the bookshop rests.
It has been a busy day, but now
the love poets can suspend their flirting
and lamenting, the war historians
enjoy a spell, however brief, of truce,
and the whole fretful assembly
of thinkers, arguers, puzzlers and storytellers
be good, lie still, and go to sleep.

Silence and alphabetical order
prevail. Once or twice in the night
some passer-by may peep
yearningly into the dark and fail
to penetrate or disturb it. The door says 'Closed',
and the door is right!

Zero Corporation Tax

Glass colludes with glass,
presents a blind and mirrored eye
to the mirrored eye across the way.

A brilliant, mid-November day,
when the sun itself is low enough
to poke its nose inside,

yet can't enlighten us, defied
by glass, spreadsheets of glass
that rise, empty of information,

high and at deflecting angles
above the hugger-mugger wards and streets.

Malala

Malala – beautiful name
and brave, beautiful spirit –
because she spoke up
and won't shut up
about her right to go to school,
has been shot in the head and neck.
Among schoolfriends. On the bus
home from school.
Head, I suppose, because she has one
and wants to use it;
neck, for its pride and grace.

She didn't die. Right now she's in hospital,
here in the UK, which we trust
is a safe and healing place.

I have thought about her, distantly
and intermittently,
much of the week.

One afternoon, schoolgirls in uniform,
freed from lessons, board my bus
like a flock of birds that, landing,
must scrap and jostle for space,
each exercising full-blast
her individual
North London teenager shriek:
more piercing than a referee's whistle!
Climbing the stairs, one aims
a reverse kick as another
tugs at her satchel

and pencils, notepads, soft toys, make-up –
stuff spills out.
There are screams and jeers,
rude words and unkind names.
Enough! Enough!

War Song for Civilians

O bombs in whom our leaders trust,
bring us your gifts of death and dust!

The minor gods of moth and rust
bow down before your greater lust.

You drop from heaven, so must be just.

Bless us now with your mighty gust,
smash roofs and walls like pastry crust,

while we stand bloodied and concussed
praising your gifts of death and dust.

A Cold Going

We're ready to leave, most of us, tonight.
Even Grandmother, who keeps her chair
close to the empty stove and insists she won't move.
Light as a hen to lift, though; and doesn't she
look like a hen, wrapped in all her clothes
and with her bony ankles jutting out!
The stove is another, heavier matter:
old, taken-for-granted family friend.
What a waste and shame to leave it behind,
yet what can we do, with every handcart in town
wheeled away weeks ago? We've been too slow –
days blown in futile haggling with those brothers
from nowhere and their imaginary lorry.
I knew the truth as soon as I felt my banknotes,
a wad as thick as a book, prised from my fingers.
'A lorry!' my clever son cried. 'Where
would the petrol have come from?' He's staying.
He has a new business: picking over the rubbish heaps.
It may lead to bigger things. He's helping us
tie our bundles now, telling us what to put in,
what to forget. Cruel decisions. The donkey
will come with us, of course, but not the goat.
Should we untether her, or would it make any difference
whether she walks into gunfire, or waits
till it comes to her? I think I'll let her die
tied to the fig-tree she knows so well.
It's a wonder the house itself has not yet been hit
by artillery fire from either side, or commandeered
by the boys in ill-assorted uniforms,
who now rush up and down our narrow lanes,
gesticulating with their weapons and shouting

in foreign accents. Praise God, we'll be gone
before any such thing happens.
Dusk already. Ice in the air. Those flashes, too,
that threaten to replace our familiar constellations.
At the agreed hour, we'll be out through the back gate.
I'll say a silent goodbye to the garden
and its pots of herbs, as we pass through.
Then eleven of us will be on our way:
Grandmother carried – complaining, no doubt –
between a pair of us; the rest trudging with our
various dreams and despairs to keep us diverted,
towards the mountains and a distant country
none of us ever wished to visit.

Argos

After years of war and wandering,
Odysseus, the island king,
arrives home. But he's in disguise,
dressed as a beggar, to surprise
the rogues who have taken
Penelope, his faithful queen,
hostage while he's been away.
So far, child's play. Nobody has seen
beyond the rags and filthy beard
to the mighty warrior they once revered.
Only when he nears his gate
does an aged dog, an itchy-looking chap
with grizzled muzzle and eyes like pebbles,
start from his snooze at the king's approach,
sniff the air and try to yap:
a noise that begins in the chest, gruff
and baritone enough, but, mid-throat,
turning to a pleading tremolo,
before whimpering out.
At which, Odysseus recognises
Argos, his favourite hound,
the hunting companion he left behind
all those years ago; and it seems
Argos knows him, for he tries to stand,
though his legs can't take the strain,
nor his heart, and he falls back again. Dead.
Odysseus has adventures ahead –
some business with a bow,
slaughter of suitors, rescue of queen –
but what I want is to pause here
and ask what this episode is meant to mean.

Another Greek Incident

Large old dog lies
at the side of the road:
he does not rise
to recognise
a long-absent master;
he does not even
open his eyes
till a rare car or truck
comes past, not especially
close or fast,
but still a provocation;
and alert at last
he raises a gruff
affronted bark,
then raises himself
with a heavy, hairy,
whole-body shrug,
and the race is on:
not too far –
though large, he's old –
but far enough
to show with a bold
broadside salvo
of gusty woofs,
and lunges and leaps
at the driver's door,
what heroic stuff
he is made of, before
the car gathers speed
and there is no further need
to chase it, pride

being satisfied;
and he can subside
once more at the side
of the road, where these days
nothing happens,
or not very much.

Morning in Giorgio's Garden

Tiny, assiduous bees
work the pomegranate trees.

Snails in a search party crawl
up the shadow side of the wall.

Spiders have sealed gaps
with cleverly engineered traps.

Birds are cooing and tweeting
at their morning briefing meeting.

My wife has taken a broom
to make the patio a tidy room.

Yoghurt and honey in a bowl
concentrate body and soul.

Encounters with Local Gods and Spirits

'Welcome,' said the Weather God.
'And here's an oratorio
for several choirs of thunder
I've composed for your arrival,
with a flamboyant light-show
for you to cringe and scurry under,
and hours and hours
of gutter-guggling showers.'

Next morning, we thanked him:
'Well, that was grand,
but we're simple folk and all we want
is steady, bland,
uncomplicated sunshine.'
'Precisely,' he replied,
'what I have planned.'

∽

We ran into the Goddess of Shopping:
'Take my advice,' she said.
'A fish market and a hardware store
are invariably worth stopping for.
Fish glistening in a slobber of ice,
the gleam on new ironmongery –
what goldsmith's work, what jewellery
can compare with these?
Buy, if you please, if you must,
if the price allows, but first
let the eye be fed.'

∽

The God of Grilled Fish
said, 'You may have any wish
so long as it's on the menu.'

Swordfish flavoured with oregano and woodsmoke,
succulent, suckered octopus tentacles
charred at their tips,
came to the table.
Wine from a bottle with no label
was raised to our lips.

'Don't forget,' the God said, 'I am also
the God of Starving Cats.'

And there, on cue, was one –
skinnymalinks and pregnant –
that mewed and wheedled at our feet.
We dropped a scrap or two, or several,
and watched her eat.

∽

Who would have thought such small waves
held such power?
Barely calf-deep, but already insecure
on a footing of uneven pebbles,
I was easily toppled.
Pushed one way, dragged the other,
I went under,
my feeble doggy-paddle no use whatsoever
against a force so turbulently playful.

Winded, snorting salt, I crawled ashore,
while all around
Sea Nymphs, sleek and buoyant
in their bathing costumes,
exulted in the favour of the Sea God,
their many-many-times-great-grandfather.

～

The Goddess of Country Nights spoke with ardour:
'While my sister, the Moon, attends to her simple duties,
collecting all the hymns and garlands in the process,
I am kept down below, in the shadows of her effulgence,
endlessly busy. My minions are not the most manageable
    lot:
capricious mosquito, whose song has little more music
than a tinnitus, farm dogs whose choral efforts
fall apart every time because they all think they're
    soloists,
donkey with his bronchial honk, shrieking, pea-brained
    peacock,
and that other cock whose aubades can occur at any
    hour
between midnight and sunrise – and do so frequently.
With material like this, do you wonder the results are
    wretched?'
We tried to console her, insisting that, far from being
    troubled,
we had been richly entertained, but she seemed not to
    believe us.

～

Indolence and swank
of yachts at the marina.

Shimmying loops of sealight
lick and tickle the hulls.

Very junior Sea Sprites
are charged with this function.

∽

Remarkably uncrumbled,
the ancient design:
each radial
and concentric line,
the fanning-out and fixity
of steep stone steps and seats,
as sternly pleasing
as they must have been
to architect and builder.
Acoustic law meets
ravishment of the eye!

Then the needling, teasing
voice of a Shade
broke in on reverie:
'This place was not made
for such prim satisfactions.
Words of terror, spilling of blood,
the catastrophic actions
of misguided mortals,

any and every
folly and outrage,
came to life here
through the art of true poets.
Now, go on your way
in trembling and fear!'

'A ruin is a building that aspires
to the ideal.' The Goddess was in lecture mode.
'Look at my own now: long released from function –
nobody praises or prays to me any more –
it stands on high ground, open to a bare, blue sky,
a structure of huge gaps held together by fragments
which men have found lying about and fumbled into
      place,
columns pocked and pitted, incomplete cross-pieces,
blocks that couldn't be accommodated pushed to the
      side like boulders:
pretty in its way and prettier by far
than the sturdy, gaudy temple they first put up to
      honour me,
but not yet the beautiful absence that might be
      achieved.
A few more millennia, though, should see to that.
I remain an optimist and, being the Goddess
who Disappeared, I have all the time in the world.'

Fennel sweetens the air.
Evening draws near
and, with it, the Goddess –
the Goddess of Herbs and Aromatics –
who whispers:
'You who believe yourselves
citizens of nowhere,
cease to be vagrant,
make this fragrant
moment your home . . .
Stay!'

from A Trip to Świder

after Konstanty Ildefons Gałczyński
and in collaboration with Renata Senktas

Stars like musicians.
August like a green bird.
The stars play. The wind dances.
And August sheds feathers.

The night keeps soaring,
a tower of silver windows.
August has mounted the tower,
its wings are beating time.

Shadows among the pines
appear and disappear.
Down the path, a proud young man
rides his motorcycle.

The moon like a puppet
has come out through a curtain of cloud.
Girls are sleeping in hammocks.
Very pretty girls.

Suddenly, from a chink in a wall,
a cricket in waltz time. Then a pause.
The girls have shifted in their hammocks.
They speak verse in their sleep.

In a cottage smothered in weeds
and with a glowworm flying over it,
an accordion from the suburbs
mourns for the death of summer.

Music happy with itself
in its anguished semitones.
The whole of Świder is there
in the sound of this accordion.

Children in prams, woodpeckers,
a birch growing at a slant,
the river, and the blind man
who drank beer at the station;

and this house with its pointed roof
hidden among raspberry bushes,
and this shadow . . . as in *Three Sisters*
by Anton Chekhov.

Prose

Prose pays a call on poetry.
A seafaring tower block,
palatial, proud, pristinely white
as if fresh from the drawing board
of some high-minded architect,
has arrived to inspect
the tired old city.
It comes as a shock:
the wash she shoulders out of the way
testing the strength of wooden piles
on which so many centuries
have improbably stood.
Docked, she commands a neighbourhood
of secretive terracotta roofs,
illogical footpaths, bridges that connect
one muddle to the next.
What does she hope to understand
of domes and doges, canals, concertos,
carnivals and churches –
all in a voluptuous sprawl
nobody planned?
What does she want? Explanations? Proofs?
Stacked rows of portholes, zeros
spelling out zillions,
peer down at the disarray below,
but, thanks to her haughty brilliance,
she is her own defensive wall
against it.
Gondolas ply to and fro,
ice creams are sold and tasted,
old art and altars take in the passing trade,

and at the end of the day –
a day snootily wasted –
announcing her resolve
with a rude hoot,
the intruder departs.

On the Road Out of Mandalay

Pre-dawn dogs,
lone dogs and dog gangs,
that our headlamps light up
lividly, unsettlingly,
like momentary spooks,
forgive us our trespass
on your ancestral territory,
the middle of the road;
but be assured also
that, having a plane to catch,
we shall pass swiftly,
happy to be forgotten by you
as a meaningless dream.

Grace

Stone that wants to run,
stone that would like to leap
and try to fly –

unmissable at the end
of the improbably long
Guildhall building on Alfred Gelder Street –

raised above the roofline
to stand as apotheosis
of all junkshop mantelpiece knickknacks,

as forerunner and out-pacer
of an entire generation's
car-bonnet figurines –

the Edwardian lass with her sky-cutting profile,
speeding drapery
and out-thrust, out-of-the-way-please trident,

who just manages
to manage her team
of untamed, same-stone horses,

on an ordinary, dullish Monday morning
catches the eye and lifts the heart
simultaneously,

as I hope she will
whenever I pass her by
on ordinary, dullish Monday mornings to come.

Ink

By mischance, I fell among the drinkers of ink.
I knew them at once by their stained lips, their sour
    stink
and the light-threatened look in their eyes, a perpetual
    half-awake blink.

In their awkward way, they were friendly at first,
offering me a bottle of ink to assuage my traveller's
    thirst.
I downed it in one gulp and nodded thanks, with my
    lips pursed.

You could get used to the taste, I thought, in time, by an
    effort of will,
but could you ever, with their apparent relish, swill
gallons of the stuff and not spend all day feeling
    vibrantly ill?

To them, however, ink was not just what water is to you
    and me;
it was a rich, nutritious broth, a soothing tea,
a courage-boosting liquor and a loving-cup of
    sacramental efficacy.

If paper was their staple diet, ink lent
distinction and purpose to their culture. A blue or black
    tongue meant
their every utterance had God's unequivocal assent.

I knew my squeamishness would be construed as pride
and hoped it would pass unnoticed, but it was too great
    to hide
and before long I was summoned to the temple to have
    my appetite tried.

Picture the wrath on the face of the high priest, with his
    indelible
beard of inky dribble,
as he watched me dip the corner of an A4 sheet and
    take a fastidious nibble.

Rising from his throne, jabbing at me with his gold-
    nibbed pen,
he pronounced instant banishment. Roused, his men
shoved and buffeted me as far as the gates, and I was
    out on the road again.

Three Academic Pastorals

Horse

Tracks that tie
town to town
leave farmland free.
From the tight-
stretched train, I see
quaint, tilted fields
flung down
haphazardly.
In one, my eye
is caught by a lone
riderless horse
taking a short
canter – on the sly,
like a loose thought.

Swan

As if from sleep,
from the nest of its own
black feathers,
the swan's neck
stirs, sways up –

a languid whip –

a barely awake
but flute-swayed snake –

loose end escaped
from the untidy
bundle of the body –

in a bid to fare
forward, which it does,
steady ahead,
with a neat naval air,
a fixed and inflexible
periscope glare.

    River

    after Ibn Sa'id

The river is
       an endless scroll
on which the breeze
       writes its wise thoughts
so trees can stoop
       and study them.

Charms of Lost Villages

Thanks to a prank of God
the fine folk of Ravenser Odd
no longer sleep under the sod
but mingle with herring and cod.

Frismersk and Saltaugh dead
turned rudely out of bed
must sleepwalk till Doomsday led
by ferry lights overhead.

Ladies of Orwithfleet
who used to be so discreet
troll down the village street
in a seaweed winding sheet.

From Turmarr to Sand le Mere
what the fishermen fear
is that corpses will swim too near
and they'll net a nose or an ear.

Wherever the tide misbehaves
opening and plundering graves
the only way anyone saves
himself is by hiding his bones in the waves.

Unruly Thoughts

after the Old Irish

Shame on my thoughts,
forever at play!
I dread what their wild sports
will bring me on Judgement Day.

During psalm-singing, they stravage
down every wrong road;
they roister, they rampage
in full sight of God.

At gatherings, at parties
of frivolous women,
through woodlands, through cities,
they go storming.

Along pleasant avenues
lightly they saunter;
down paths not in common use,
I tell you, they blunder.

Without a boat, they can hop
across the wide ocean;
in one bound, fly up
from earth to heaven.

Afraid of nothing,
they foolishly roam,
then from their profligate outings
scamper back home.

Though you try to constrain them
or shackle their feet,
they lack the discipline
to keep still and be quiet.

Neither blade nor flail
will cow them – more sinuous
than eels' tails
slipping through my fingers.

Neither lock nor dungeon
nor iron chain,
neither moat nor bastion
will make them refrain.

Dear Christ, in your chastity
and all-seeing wisdom,
may your sevenfold ministry
help me resist them.

Take command of my heart,
God who made all,
till I love you as I ought
and do your will.

Admit me, Christ,
to your blessed company,
you who are true and worthy of trust –
unlike me.

A Kilnsea Chorale

The Kapellmeister of Kilnsea
confronts his mutinous choir.

He has a new cantata that he wants them to sing,
but they have a composition of their own

that they're in the middle of now,
and they're not about to interrupt it:

a chorale of absolute din, a multitude-part
white-noise polyphony, almost unhearable

upwhelming basso-profundities
supporting a shoving and tumbling

scrum of unresolved counterpoint
with, at the top, a foamy descant, all ecstatic shatters.

They won't stop. But the Kapellmeister
is patient. His cantata can wait.

It may even be improved, if he listens with care
and can catch and steal whatever it is

that gives the racket its seeming power and purpose,
and slip it into the neat score on his desk at home.

The Isle of Relleu

for Christopher and Marisa North

Not Circe's island, but that of her distant cousin,
    perhaps.
An enchantress, certainly, watches over these crags and
    terraces.
Orchard trees, whose delight is to dream up oranges,
almonds and pomegranates, attest to her benign
    governance.
Lightning, the gentlest electrical flicker at night,
and the fitful barking of farm dogs by day
speak to us, who have reached here – by whatever
    route –
of the possibility, if not the full achievement,
of arrival and belonging. The one big question is what
    to do
with all this easy beauty. Which is why we assemble
    each morning
indoors at a plain wooden table, with notebooks and
    frowns,
to puzzle over, to pick at, and to pronounce on poetry:
that art with no answer, words meant to muddle
    meaning,
music that mystifies. Meanwhile, the Sun, our
    enchantress's
elderly father, takes the constitutional that he considers
a full-time job; the orange-trees add to their already
hand's-stretch-challenging clusters of fruit; and the sky
    decides
what shade of blue it will be today, for dogs to bark at
and poets to try to describe.

Granada in Noise and Music

for Róisín

Agua! Agua! The dog across the street
tells us he's thirsty, but we don't believe
a word of it. His role is to repeat,
and ours, no less a duty, to receive
this morning mantra, valid only for
its emptiness of meaning. Distant dogs
echo and amplify his lone uproar,
till a polyphony of monologues –
random, discordant, free of beat or measure –
unites all districts of the waking city.
Cocks in back yards contribute at their leisure
from throats that, to my ears, sound parched and gritty.
            Listen, my love: this out-of-tunefulness
            is ours to share, and we will share it. Yes?

Loud traffic, street crowds, trash music from bars:
downtown at evening is so frankly raucous,
it can be hard to recollect that Lorca's
fastidious lyrics with their weeping guitars,
green winds, blue horses, Gypsy moons and blood,
sprang from this city. Which you like to call
a country town, not just because it's small,
but for its manners – gruff, grounded, and good.
Lorca himself, a social creature, had
a bar he liked, closed now. I expect the place
met him each time with much the same embrace
of shouty talk as makes you and me glad,

stepping into some old haunt full of folk
noisily sharing the big human joke.

∽

Sweet, wheedling melody and squodgy chords:
the stolid street accordionist gives vent
to a lachrymosity too deep for words.
Fleet fingerwork allows him to absent
his private thoughts, if any; his face remains
unreadable, for either poetry or prose.
Piaf he isn't, pumping out the strains
of her perennial *La Vie en rose*
for the nth time today; and yet it seems
to do the job. When he takes round his cup –
his reasonable message being that dreams
cost money – table by table we cough up.
      Almost as soon as he has disappeared,
      enter Bob Dylan in dreadlocks and beard.

∽

Remember our first night at the Tabanco?
El Niño de las Almendras, of whom
we'd never heard, was on. Local Flamenco
legend. His audience filled the tiny room.
Pepe (to his two female friends) was tiny
also; grey-suited, with a pink gardenia
in his buttonhole; brown brogues natty and shiny.
The young guitarist (Pepe being his senior

by fifty years) was fine; but the old man, growing
impatient with his frantic filigree,
at one point took a swipe at that too-flowing
right hand, so he himself could bawl freely.
　　　　After each song, he jumped out of his chair,
　　　　stamped feet, roared like a wild beast, punched
　　　　　the air.

∿

A man of utmost piety and creator
of gorgeous, savage scores for the ballet,
a near-recluse who served avant-garde theatre,
Manuel de Falla lived out of the way
by the Alhambra: paradoxes that please
enormously. Stravinsky, the old cat,
remembered him as prone to fall to his knees
whenever he got half a chance, but at
the same time held the work in high regard.
Visitors find the house, a hillside shrine,
immaculate and bijou, but it's hard
not to feel heavy-footed, toeing the line
　　　　from relic to relic. What's to be said
　　　　about a shut upright piano, a made bed?

∿

Clapping of hands: magical invocation
to a stand-offish dancer. Clappers clap
patterns of rhythm too sly for notation
as if to hypnotise her into the trap

of dancing. She is tentative at first,
takes a few indecisive steps, to, fro,
before her hard high heels succumb to a burst
of their own percussion, and we watch her go –
like the clappers! The guitarist joins in,
slapping both strings and wood of his guitar,
supplementing the ecstasy with din.
An everynight scene in some tourist bar?
  Oh, be wary of the tricks the mind employs,
  presuming to tell the music from the noise.

  ~

Good talk around a tapas-laden table
goes far too fast for me, a poet lost
in absence of translation, so unable
to do much more than quibble with old Frost.
And yet it's fun: catching one word in five,
then dropping it in haste to catch the next,
feels quite a lively way to be alive –
not least in this particular context,
where I can sit back and admire how you,
a poet needing no translation, exchange
quick-witted Spanish with old friends and new,
making a music both your own and strange.
  Let language share our month-long holiday
  in noise and music, poetry and play!

Trees of Cádiz

The superpurple of the jacarandas
against a pale-blue sky
outpurples purple itself.

Heroic, elephantine Moreton Bay figs
dangle new roots
above unwatered soil.

In the plaza, marine-breeze-tattered palm trees
form ranks with lampposts
to create a civic glade.

Cypresses, clipped to cylinders and spirals,
crowd shoulder to shoulder
and snub the prying sun.

¡Árboles de Cádiz! así ustedes vigilan
orgullosamente
la alma de su gente.

Pueblo Natal

Gitanos y perros
y nada de sombra
en Fuente Vaqueros,
donde la luz de sol
encombra
pesadamente
el espíritu del infante
Federico García Lorca,
que, en su cuña
desocupada
y adornada
con chucherías inmensas,
exclama, «¡Quiero salir
de este pueblo natal
y convertirme
en poeta
de reputación mundial!»

At a Procession

The Virgin is coming
and, when she comes,
she will come to the drumming
of Spanish drums.

She will come to the braying
of Spanish brass;
in shuffling order,
the brass bands pass.

Be patient, be patient,
as each band comes
with tormented trumpets
and punished drums.

Drums thump the midriff,
brass scourges the ear –
and still the Virgin
is nowhere near.

But never stop praying
that she is coming:
believe the braying,
put faith in the drumming!

The Late Sun

I note from the obituaries that the Sun,
the legendary cinematographer,
has died. His work was highly regarded
in the business. J. M. W. Turner said,
'The Sun is God' – and you could see he meant it.
The French school, too – the Impressionists –
could hardly have achieved their revolution
without his technical savoir faire. Among poets,
Wallace Stevens voiced the most profuse
and frequent tributes, but I have reasons of my own
for gratitude. One morning, in particular,
in Granada, as I sipped coffee on my balcony,
he lit the dawn for me. His art was both
panoramic and minutely detailed.
First, he touched in a mountain to the left,
giving it a deep, umber, emberishly unsteady glow,
before moving on to the sky, from which he suggested
other mountains in shades of dark grey and indigo
so little different – mountains of air
shaped from a stony sky – that it seemed uncertain
how such indeterminacies could resolve;
though they did, in time, in full clarity and vastness.
None of this happened in a hurry. It was all
gradual and considered. To watch was to take
a lesson in light and being alive. Which I have tried to
     learn.
Only the death notices, coming so prematurely,
have dashed my spirits more than they usually do.
It's plain that, not just I, but the whole world
should have paid closer attention while he was still
     working.

Acknowledgements

My warmest thanks to the editors of *About Larkin*, *Archipelago*, *Areté*, *The Compass*, the *Dark Horse*, *Drift* and *Spear's*, where some of these poems were first printed; to Clutag Press and Rack Press, publishers, respectively, of the booklets *Clutag Five Poems No. 3* and *Yesterday's News*, where other poems have appeared; to Alain de Botton, who prompted and generously subsidised the writing of *Yesterday's News*; to Jen Campbell, who commissioned 'Bookshop at Night' for her celebration of the world's great bookshops, *The Bookshop Book*; to Renata Senktas, with whom I worked for some happy months on a translation of Konstanty Ildefons Gałczyński's 'Wycieczka do Świder' ('A Trip to Świder'); to the poet's daughter, Kira Gałczyńska, for allowing me to include an excerpt from that translation here; and to Maurice Riordan, who invited me to translate 'Unruly Thoughts' for his anthology of early Irish poetry, *The Finest Music*, supplying the crib that enabled me to do so. Some other poems were in *A Box of Tricks for Anna Zyx*, distributed privately by my own press, Ondt & Gracehoper.